Marriage Hints
for *LDS Newlyweds*

Marriage Hints
for *LDS Newlyweds*

Amy Martinsen

WALNUT SPRINGS PRESS

ISBN-13: 978-1-59992-212-6

Printed in the United States of America

Contents

Introduction

The morning sun shone brightly through the east window of the sealing room—almost as brightly as the faces of the bride and groom. They were a beloved young couple, so it was standing room only. Beloved, yes, but they also had a General Authority performing their sealing. No one wanted to miss the sage marriage advice that would surely preface the sacred ordinance. As he began to speak, we all leaned in.

He had no marriage advice, he told the couple. How could he possibly give that sort of advice with his wife sitting a few chairs away, and him having yet to master the simple task of picking up his socks? Go buy a book for that, he told the couple, with a smile. Then he said, "But let's take a few moments and talk about the temple covenants."

I'm with the General Authority on this one—giving marriage advice would be the last thing I'd want to do. In fact, the idea of setting myself up as an expert on marriage makes me queasy. There is so much I don't know . . . and yet I've been asked to write this book.

So, I'm not going to tell you what to do in the beginning of your marriage. That's up to you. Perhaps, though, this book can give you ideas, raise questions, and make you laugh. And, as the kind General Authority did for all of us on that beautiful morning, turn our heads toward the temple and the covenants we make there—and encourage us to live them.

Still, a few hints here and there can't hurt, right?

1

The Questions Change

For weeks the questions were easy and fun. What theme are you using for your reception? What color of ties are the men wearing? Are you using succulents in your bouquet, or going with the woodsy look? The future groom politely stepped aside as the bride-to-be flicked through pictures on her phone, her fingers a blur above the dozens of photos from Pinterest and Instagram. He watched adoringly as she showed the questioner images of chalkboard signs, mossy slabs of wood, and chiffon-draped ceilings.

But now that you're married, the questions have changed dramatically. And they are directed to the both of you—no stepping aside allowed. Are you both working? Are you both in school? What are your career plans? What kind of salary does that pay? And the big kahuna of all questions: when will you start your family? Church culture seems to almost demand that we quiz newlyweds on these personal matters. Most people mean well and just want to help you along the path they've already trod. We are a church centered on growth and progress. We'll make sure you keep moving and growing, even if you've only been married for a week. In fact, we'll ask a good number of these questions as we congratulate you in your reception line. You're probably getting the idea that these questions can't be avoided no matter how hard you try, but perhaps with a well-practiced plan, they can be cut short. For example, the wife can shuffle in her bag for the needed paperwork while the husband enthusiastically gives his sales pitch for the multi-level business "everyone will want in on." At that point, the questioning should end abruptly.

2

About Those Gift Cards

You made a haul at your reception—registry items, gift cards, and lots of cash. Literally overnight, you've gone from having to scrimp and save, to owning a large lump of loot. But who gets to spend the lump, and how? This can go many different ways. Your spouse may want to hoard the gift cards and put the cash toward student loans, while you may have visions of heading straight to where Chip and Joanna Gaines have taken up residence in Target. Your reception guests were kind and generous, and many of them gave you what you want most—the chance to choose your own gifts. So, choose, but choose together. You and I both know, though, that it will be better all the way around if the wife gets the Target gift cards.

3

Playing the Waiting Game

You and your spouse have smashed down the garbage so efficiently, a garbage compactor would be envious. Then you start stacking—the empty box teetering on the edge of the trash can, crowded by the wads of paper towels next to the paper plates folded into quarters but threatening to pop back to their full size. Just when you think nothing else could possibly fit in the garbage can, your spouse builds a new platform with a frozen pizza box . . . and the stacking continues. It's an engineering feat, yet someone's got to give in and take out the trash.

This isn't really about garbage—it's about who does what. And if you don't talk about it, the resentment will stack higher than the nested take-out containers. Every time you walk by the overflowing garbage can, it will call out to you, begging you to get down to the nitty-gritty of what's going on here, because things aren't smelling so good.

Maybe your wife's dad always took out the garbage, so your wife never had to think about it. Or your husband's mom always made him take it out and he hates doing it. Whatever the case, all the situation needs is a little discussion and perhaps a joke or two. Because constructing a Mount Everest of garbage takes much more effort than simply taking out the garbage.

4

Money and Those Warehouse Clubs: A Cautionary Tale

You've probably heard it before: "Try to walk out of one of those warehouse clubs without spending a hundred dollars." Are people who say this overspenders with no self-discipline? You're not sure, but you've been given a six-month membership as a wedding gift, so you and your spouse decide to go see what it's all about. You allot yourselves forty dollars and smugly flash your shiny red-white-and-blue card to the employee at the club's entrance.

The first thing you see is a portable go-anywhere charcoal grill with all the bells and whistles. It would be perfect for the patio area of your apartment, not to mention trips to the lake. It's twice the amount of your budget, though, so you walk on by, but not before you catch a whiff of grilled meat. Is this part of the display? Maybe it's coming from the food court. Your stomach growls and you look at your spouse. Neither of you ate before you came here — the plan was to do a fast-food drive-through on the way home. It probably wasn't such a good idea to come here hungry.

For strength, you take hold of your loved one's hand—easy, because you didn't get a shopping cart. Forty dollars' worth of stuff would hardly warrant a cart, let alone one of those ridiculous flatbed things. With a fresh surge of self-control, you fling a mocking glance back at the go-anywhere grill and almost run smack-dab into a pallet of chocolate-covered pretzels. You and your new spouse love these things. The huge bags are the same price as the small ones in the grocery store. And these are just a few dollars, really. You pick up a bag of the pretzels and cradle it in your arm as your spouse agrees it's an affordable treat.

You continue to the produce section, which you've heard is great. But to get there you must negotiate the deli section. Sample stations are everywhere, and you cave in at the smells. A woman holding a tray of small plastic cups offers one to each of you—jalapeno-artichoke dip on a cracker. You're not going to be one of those people who shamelessly fill up on samples as if it's mealtime, but there's no need to be rude to this sweet old lady. She's just doing her job. You and your spouse each take a dip-covered cracker and eat it. The stuff is like ambrosia! Silently, something in the universe shifts. You hand your wife the affordable bag of pretzels and offer to go get a cart. She nods and heads toward the refrigerated-dip section.

An hour later, the two of you are sweaty and your stomachs are pleasantly full of samples—meatballs covered in roasted pineapplehabanero sauce, taquitos smothered in mango salsa, and several miniature smoked sausages. As you strain to maneuver your bulging cart into the checkout line, you look longingly at a person across the way with a flatbed. If you had gotten one of those instead of the shopping cart, the two-quart jar of roasted green chilis wouldn't be smashing your chicken-salad roll-ups.

When the checkout person announces your total of $246.18, you refuse to make eye contact with your spouse. All you can do is swipe your credit card and admit your resolve was no match against a double-chocolate muffin the size of a human head. Thankfully you had the presence of mind to get the package of 101 neon-colored bungee cords. You'll need some to strap the go-anywhere grill to the top of your Prius.

The moral of this cautionary tale: if you're going to one of those membership-only warehouse stores, plan on spending at least a hundred dollars. And for the love of all that is good, don't go hungry.

5

Communication: Mind Reading Doesn't Work

Not long after my husband and I were married, I attended a friend's baby shower. It was a large gathering, and while I was there a woman I barely knew said some hurtful things to me. I felt horrible and couldn't wait to get home, sure my husband would know just the right words to make me feel better. As soon as I came in the door, I went straight to him and gushed out the whole ugly experience. He looked at me, said he was sorry I felt bad, then turned and went out the back door. Bewildered, I watched as he strode purposefully out to the garden and began weeding.

Needless to say, the whole scene had played out differently in my head. Sadly, I had done what many of us do—assumed my spouse could read my mind. For some reason, we have this mistaken notion that if our husband or wife truly loves us, he or she will instinctively know what we need and want. That notion needs to go away and be replaced with something much healthier—clear and open communication. In other words, sometimes we need to actually *ask* for what we need. It may feel awkward to say the words "I need . . ." but do it anyway because it will take you to a safer place in your relationship. If you don't, you will end up stomping down these words, and we all know stomped-down words just get louder and eventually angry. It's best to say them when they are filled with love and maybe a little frustration, but not anger.

So how did the bridal-shower-garden-weeding incident play out? I admit I wanted to take a container of ice cream and a spoon out to the front porch and eat fourteen servings while I cried. But I realized that my husband shows his love through service, and at that moment he was doing what he thought would make me feel better—weeding the garden.

I fixed him a large glass of ice water, went out to where he was acting like a human rototiller, and thanked him. Then I told him I needed to talk for a bit and asked if he would listen. "Of course," he said. He pulled two lawn chairs into the shade, we sat down, and he gave me his full attention while I spilled my guts. Was it uncomfortable asking my new husband to listen to me? Yes. But it would have felt much worse packing on a few pounds as I cried my way through a half gallon of Pralines and Cream on the front porch. And more importantly, it helped put my spouse and me in that safe place where we can ask each other for what we need. I may have still eaten some ice cream, but with a much healthier motive.

6

Saving—That Beautiful Sound of Cold, Hard Cash

It's hard to save money when you don't have much. And a lack of money naturally leads to fear. As you lay awake late at night, the fear will whisper, "What if we have a car accident? What if one of us loses our job? What if we get sick?" Fear, or even panic, will ride along to the store with you, reminding you of all the things you want and need but can't afford. You and your spouse may even turn on each other because of the financial stress. Money, and the lack thereof, is one of Satan's favorite tools for creating a wedge between husbands and wives. But as the Apostle Paul said, "God hath not given us the spirit of fear; but of power, and of love, and of a sound mind" (2 Timothy 1:7).

This verse can apply to many aspects of life, but I have experienced its empowerment in saving money, even when my husband and I were desperately poor. We had a large water jug, the kind with the narrow neck, and every few days we'd drop in our spare change—a dime, a nickel, or even pennies. The money made a wonderful clinking sound as it landed in the jug. I think Lucy described it best when she collected a nickel from Charlie Brown for her psychiatric help and dropped it in her money jar: "Boy, what a sound. How I love hearing that old money clink. That beautiful sound of cold, hard cash . . . that beautiful sound of clinking nickels" (*A Charlie Brown Christmas*, CBS, 1965).

It felt good to put coins in the money jug, as our children called it, because my husband and I were standing up against fear. We were exercising faith, taking action to make our circumstances better, even a few pennies at a time. Then we could kneel in prayer and confidently ask for help—a better job, cars that didn't break down, good health. As we acted in faith, a blessing came that we hadn't expected: a sound mind. We had peace. Our financial problems didn't magically go away, but we could think straight, have order in our actions, be kind to and close to each other, and no longer live in fear.

That jug of money, which Rick and I have filled and emptied several times, paid for our car insurance and property taxes, several emergencies, and eventually, a few trips to Disneyland. We have since developed different (and interest-bearing) ways of saving, but we've kept the money jug. Our children grew up contributing to it and watching the coins pile up. When they'd drop in a few coins, they'd recite Lucy's mantra, "How I love hearing that money clink." Maybe she *was* offering psychiatric help to Charlie Brown, by letting him hear the sound of saved money and what it does for the soul. I believe it is wise counsel—priceless, even.

7

Taking Your Place at the Helm

Dietrich Bonhoeffer advised his soon-to-be-married niece that in marriage you take your place "at a post of responsibility towards the world and mankind" (Dietrich Bonhoeffer, *Letters and Papers from Prison*, ed. Eberhard Bethge [Minneapolis, Minnesota: Fortress Press, 1953], 42–43). For newlyweds, that doesn't sound like much fun. But it can be.

I like to think of this "post of responsibility" as the helm of a large ship. You and your spouse stand side by side at the helm. Your ship may be small now, and it may be just the two of you on board, but regardless, you are at the helm. Now you decide what to load onto your ship. Here's where it gets fun. This is your marriage ship, and you two are in charge. Want to paint it purple and yellow? Great. Decide you want it blue instead? Repaint it. Is there some stuff that's not working for you? Chuck it overboard . . .

literally. It's all up to you. But whatever this cargo is, it will show the world what marriage means to you.

Will your ship be a ship of service, of peace, of love? Will there be unity, kindness, and clear communication? Will laughter ring out? Will others feel safe on your ship? And will people look at both of you standing at the helm and think, "I want that kind of happiness"? Only you and your spouse can answer these questions. But as your ship fills and life happens and you hit some rough waters, remember something else Dietrich Bonhoeffer told his niece: "In marriage you are a link in the chain of the generations" (ibid).

You and your spouse are not the only couples who stand at the helm of a ship. You stand with generations of other husbands and wives who took the post of responsibility to show the world what marriage can be. Show them it can be fun.

8

The Check-In and Thank You

They say if someone appreciates what you do, you can't do it fast enough. It's true. We all want to feel appreciated, but how exactly does that play out in your busy new life with your spouse? My husband and I have come up with something that works well for us, and maybe it will work for you. Desperately trying to keep ahead of five children and my husband's growing business, he and I developed a habit of checking in with each other throughout the day—who talked to whom, who needs what, who did what, etc. Just a quick glance at each other's day to keep both of us on the same page. And then we'd thank each other.

Now, we pretty much did the same things every day. My husband went to work, then did chores around the house. I drove kids to school and activities, ran endless errands, cooked, and I guarantee you, I did laundry every single day. But it felt so nice to have my husband thank me for it. This simple expression of gratitude lifted me and broke the monotony of running a home and taking care of a family. It definitely took the edge off the daily grind of laundry. And I could see the boost it gave him to be thanked for the work he did to provide for us and care for our home.

This check-in and thank you is a small thing that just takes a few minutes. And even though my husband and I are now down to one child at home—and I do much less laundry—we still carry on with this habit. Not only does it make for smoother-running days, it helps my husband and me feel that what we do every day, no matter how small and mundane, is noticed and appreciated. We all need to feel that way.

9

Mean Words and Forgiveness

An English actor and writer named Peter Ustinov said, "Love is an act of endless forgiveness, a tender look which becomes a habit."

Although I grew up in the Church and knew the principle of forgiveness, I didn't really understand it until I was married. I had read the scriptures and heard talks, but never *got* what forgiveness was until I really received it from another human being. Many times I had offered forgiveness, claiming everything was okay even though that person had hurt me. But then for days afterward I'd find ways to make the offender pay—because he or she needed to pay (yes, this thinking is really messed up).

Then one day I said something to my new husband that obviously hurt him deeply, and everything shifted. I loved him so much that the regret was unbearable. I yearned to take back the mean words I had said. I felt physically ill, and my heart ached to have things go back to the moment before I had opened my big mouth. And when I expressed all of this to my husband—through much snot and tears— he took me in his arms and said everything was all right. He meant it, too, because from that moment on, he treated me as if I had never said those horrible things. If anything, he gave me *more* love and tenderness. He did what Nephi did with his brothers, Laman and Lemuel—my husband "frankly forgave" me (1 Nephi 7:21).

Of course, saying stupid, hurtful things to one's spouse isn't as serious as what Laman and Lemuel did to Nephi—using cords to tie him up, then leaving him in the wilderness where they hoped he would be eaten by wild animals. Nephi set the bar for forgiveness pretty high with that one. Yet, he loved his family, so he offered them forgiveness, just like Heavenly Father does for us. When my husband forgave me, it was as if I had miraculously gone back to the moments before I said the mean words, as if the mean words never happened. The relief was indescribable. I understood what forgiveness really was, and I wanted to give it back to him and my family.

Some things may be easy to forgive and some may take time, but if we, like Peter Ustinov so perfectly stated, allow forgiveness to become a habit as easy as a tender look, our marriage relationship will be infinitely sweeter.

10

The Cruise Director in Your Marriage

In case you've never been on a cruise and are unfamiliar with the role of cruise director, allow me to explain it from the marriage vantage point. The cruise director is the person who plans all the fun things—parties, trips, holidays, and date nights. This person takes care of the details, gauging travel time and making reservations. He or she buys and wraps gifts, arranges babysitters, and knows how dressy to dress. This person has the answer to "Where should we eat tonight?" And he or she gets you to where you want to be.

Let's pause for a moment and be grateful we live in a time where a magical voice on our phones tells us how to get where we're going. I spent many a family vacation reading a map, usually incorrectly, from the passenger side of our minivan. Navigator is not a fun or popular job. And navigating is a major part of being cruise director. The person who invented Google Maps was really out to save relationships.

In some marriages, the role of cruise director is bounced back and forth between the spouses like a floaty pink beach ball. The wife takes charge of parties and holidays, while the husband plans trips and dates. Most of the time, though, the large responsibility of fun-maker falls to one spouse—and having to take full responsibility for such things isn't that much fun.

Whichever way you decide to divide up all that goes into a good time, it might help to remember a few things. A party with food and gifts and treats doesn't just happen. The perfectly choreographed trip of sightseeing and hikes balanced with days at the beach takes careful planning. The Christmas Eve when everyone feels the Spirit so strongly they refer to it as their favorite family time, took weeks to put together.

I will always be grateful for the advice of a dear friend when I got married. She said the experiences that make up the fun, memorable, favorite moments of our lives usually require a ton of work by the cruise director. And for it all to come to fruition, the Holy Ghost has to be there, which means the husband and wife have to be on the same page. This has proven true time and again. So be kind to whichever spouse takes up the role of cruise director. In fact, gush with appreciation, then take him or her on a luxury cruise.

11

Changing Each Other: A Slow Donkey Ride Through Hades

Marjorie Pay Hinckley said, "Early on I realized it would be better if we worked harder at getting accustomed to one another than constantly trying to change each other—which I discovered was impossible . . . There must be a little give and take, and a great deal of flexibility, to make a happy home" (Virginia H. Pearce, ed. *Glimpses into the Life and Heart of Marjorie Pay Hinckley* [Salt Lake City, UT: Deseret Book Co., 1999], 184, 186).

I loved Sister Hinckley. Her outlook on life was real, and her sense of humor was clever and delightful. I like to imagine her and President Gordon B. Hinckley trying to change each other. That had to be interesting. My attempts to change my husband, and his attempts to change me, have proven to be the equivalent of a long, sweaty, miserable donkey ride through Hades. And impossible.

I don't know what it is that makes us feel we need to—or have the power to—change another person. I believe the spouse wanting to do the changing feels justified and well-meaning; someone has to save the other person from himself or herself. But the one being changed always feels not good enough . . . and that's not a good thing.

It would be so much better to spend our time and energy "getting accustomed" to each other. This phrase sounds as if you are getting to know your spouse for the first time. And in some ways, you are. Living together, making a home together, and deciding your future together is much different than courtship. There are bound to be some surprises. Pray to see the strengths in these surprises and seek to find ways to be flexible. Then the "give and take" will happen, and that's so much better than a sweaty donkey ride. Trust me on this.

12

Humor and Confidence

Most people don't immediately associate confidence with humor, but that connection can be pivotal in choosing what kind of humor you want to have in your marriage. And you've got to have some humor. It can build and bind and get you through some rough spots.

President Gordon B. Hinckley said, "Everywhere is heard the snide remark, the sarcastic gibe, the cutting down of associates" (Gordon B. Hinckley, "The Continuing Pursuit of Truth," *Ensign*, Apr. 1986). We all know someone who takes the cheap shot, whose attempts at being funny are always at another person's expense. The "sarcastic gibe" is easy to take and it gets laughs, but in the end it makes the "teaser" look bad instead of clever and popular. Humor that builds and binds can in a moment turn into something equally destructive and hurtful—sarcasm.

I believe giving into the siren of sarcasm comes from a lack of confidence, among other things. It feels good to make others laugh, to have that moment in the spotlight, but never if it hurts someone. Especially if that someone is your spouse.

There are all kinds of humor—the good-spirited teasing, the self-deprecating wit, the laugh-out-loud irony. The list is long, but every type of humor can cross the line to hurtful sarcasm in a blink of an eye. It takes a confident person to resist the temptation of sarcasm and let the cheap laugh go unsaid. The truly funny person will look for humor that lifts and that is inclusive, drawing people together, and that does the very best thing humor can do—make us laugh at ourselves. This is what you want in your marriage.

13

Disenchanted Moments

I asked several long-time married couples what advice they would give their newlywed selves if they could go back in time. Each offered several nuggets of wisdom, but literally every couple said that husbands and wives will fall in love again and again over the years. They all agreed there will be days when you aren't exactly enchanted with each other and that this is normal, so just allow yourselves to be reminded why you fell in love. A great poet wrote, "New love is the brightest and long love is the greatest. But revived love is the tenderest thing known on earth" (Thomas Hardy, *The Hand of Ethelberta* [London: Penguin Books Ltd., 1995], 182).

As a single college student, I read this quote and laughed at Hardy's use of the word "revived," thinking it sounded as if the dying love had been given CPR. My idealizing young self vowed to never have a love that needed reviving. My love would be impervious to this. But I was dead wrong.

We are all mortal, and we all have bad days. And we all have times when the spouse we are looking at barely resembles the spouse we married. This is where the reviving comes in. Maybe it will take some kindness and forgiveness—perhaps even a defibrillator, complete with shock paddles. But if you allow yourselves to fall in love over and over again, letting the Spirit bring to your minds what first drew you to each other, you will truly have a love that is the tenderest thing you know.

14

What Happens When You Pray Together

Everyone will tell you and your new spouse to pray together, but what really happens when you do? And how does it happen? Perhaps you've already made a habit of praying together before you were married, but now you're living together and it may feel different. When will you have couple's prayer, and who announces that it's time to pray? Do you take turns saying the prayer? Where will you pray? All these questions will need to be answered and may be uncomfortable at first. I don't know how, but it will all work out.

What I do know is what happens when you pray together. When you pray together, you are kneeling before Heavenly Father. You and your husband or wife are in the same posture as you were when you knelt over the altar in the temple to be sealed. You are at the same level—no one is higher or lower. Your eyes are even. Perhaps you hold hands. You held hands when you were sealed, remember? When you pray together, you ask Heavenly Father for help, for blessings, for inspiration, and safety. You will feel His Spirit, and Heavenly Father will bless you as He did that day in the temple. You and your spouse are in supplication to the Father, as you were on the day you were given the most magnificent promises together, if you are faithful to the end.

So, what happens when you pray together is that you are reminded of those moments over the altar when you were sealed to one another. If you're having a bad day, a disenchanted moment, or your marriage ship has sailed into rough waters, kneel down together and let yourselves be reminded of the best day ever.

15

Family Home Evening — It's Just What You Do

Some families seem to serve others as effortlessly as they breathe. I am convinced they have a secret bat phone like Batman on which they receive news of needs in their neighborhood before anyone else, even a really good Relief Society president and bishop. These families are there, seeing, assessing, and doing what needs to happen. They have made service a part of the culture of their family—it's just what they do. The same can happen with family home evening.

We've been commanded to hold family home evening each week. We've been promised amazing blessings if we do, and we've been given copious amounts of ideas for how to do it. But what does FHE look like when there's just the two of you? Does it feel weird and premature? Should you just wait until you have children? Yes, it may feel a bit strange. And no, don't wait, because you want this to be a part of the culture of your family. But that takes work and time.

At some point, this bat-phone family was just a husband and a wife. And at some point—no matter how small and awkward the effort—they made the choice to serve and they did it consistently. You can make that same choice with family home evening. And someday your children and family and friends will see you as that family who gathers once a week to reconnect and lift each other. It's just what you do.

16

Get the Green Bowl

"Go get the green bowl" were words no one in my family wanted to hear. It meant you were sick and could not be trusted because you might vomit on something important. It was a dreaded walk of shame into the kitchen to rummage through the cupboard to find the one-and-only green plastic bowl to be your constant companion until you could be trusted again. "Aim for the bowl" was my mother's warning cry. As you carried the green bowl around, the rest of the family would watch you as if you were a volcano about to erupt. Truth be told, you were exactly that. And if anyone forgot, there was the green bowl to remind them. It didn't help matters when everyone's fears came true and you actually erupted. This was always followed by a glass of 7-Up, which was supposed to help but would usually cause round 2 of eruptions. To this day I refuse to own anything made of green plastic and can't walk past 7-Up in the grocery store without feeling nauseous.

This was my perspective of being sick. It wasn't all green bowls and 7-Up. I was also allowed to stay home from school and watch whatever I wanted on TV. And I was given extra attention which, for a child, is always great. If I was seriously ill, Mom took me to the doctor. So, when our children were sick, I did a version of this to care for them. My husband, on the other hand, grew up on a farm located miles away from any type of medical care. His mother tended to almost all of the family's illnesses and injuries, at which she was quite gifted. You had to be really bad off to warrant a trip to the doctor, let alone lounging about the house dragging around a green plastic bowl. It was a different time and different circumstances. Knowing we had dissimilar perspectives, my husband and I would counsel together when illnesses came, deciding what would be the best and wisest care for each other and our children.

What happened in your home when you were sick? Was a green bowl strapped to your chest while everyone watched you with fearful anticipation? Or did you bind your wounds with baling wire so you could finish plowing the field? Hopefully it was something in between these two approaches. Whatever it was, talk about it with your spouse so that when illness strikes—which, unfortunately, it will—you will understand each other. It's no fun being sick, but it's a little easier if there's someone there to help you the way you're used to being helped.

By the way, you would be amazed what I can do with baling wire.

17

Retirement and Magic Advice from the Future

In the movie *Frequency* (New Line Cinema, 2000), the main character, John, is able to talk to his dad over thirty years earlier, via a special short-wave radio. In more of these time-travel conversations, he speaks to his younger self and to his best friend, Gordo. Haven't we all wanted to give advice to our younger selves? Each time I watch this movie, I cry when adult John gives encouragement to young John. And then I laugh when adult John, as a last thought, gives young Gordo some magical advice—to invest in Yahoo! At the end of the movie, adult Gordo is driving an expensive sports car with the word "Yahoo!" on the personalized license plate, so we know he took his friend's advice from the future.

I can't help but think how nice it would've been to have some mystery person give me sure-fire financial advice for my future. Well, here I am and here's the magic advice to you: save for retirement now. Some of your busiest years are ahead of you, and they will pass before you know it. Make a plan now, even if retirement seems a million miles away. I promise you, it's not that far.

Educate yourselves. Take a class. Avail yourselves of the financial courses available through your stake employment specialist (that would make a great FHE, but only if you go out for ice cream afterwards—that's a thing, you know). Take action now and be ahead of the game so that retirement doesn't have a chance to surprise you. You probably won't be as successful as young Gordo with his Yahoo! insight, but you'll be prepared . . . and that will feel magical.

18

Kindness—Little Things and What They Build

It may be cliché to say that kindness is about the little things—the kind little acts we do for each other. I want to take it a step further and look at what all those little acts build. The Lord has told us, "And out of small things proceedeth that which is great" (Doctrine and Covenants 64:30). Usually this scripture is used as an example of how to build great character and spiritual strength, but it is also how we build love.

You can tell when someone is genuinely being kind to you. The act of kindness has your comfort and happiness at its center and is not on display for others to admire. You can feel the love in it because all the giver wants is your happiness. To the giver, the act of kindness may seem small, but to you—the one receiving it—it feels anything but small. It swells your heart.

You may know a couple who have been married for many years. It is clear they belong with each other by the way they *are* together. They instinctively touch each other—a tap on the shoulder, a squeeze of the hand. They catch each other's eye and can't help but smile. They laugh together. This couple is kind to each other in small ways and big. But I guarantee you it's the small, daily, heart-swelling acts of kindness that only they see that have made this kind of togetherness. They've built a great love, one small act of kindness at a time. And you can too.

19

The Completeness of the Temple

I hope everyone who reads this book has a desire to attend the temple. I don't in any way want to be exclusionary. If you haven't yet gone to the temple, please work with your bishop and stake president so you can go. The work we do in the temple—providing saving ordinances for the dead—is one reason we are here on earth. Sealing families together is where it's at when it comes to mortality. And please remember, if only perfect people were allowed in the temple, it would be an empty building. The Lord wants you in His house.

There's a completeness you feel in the temple. It's unlike anything else you'll ever experience. You are helping to complete an eternal chain, each link bringing all of us closer to the day when the Lord declares that our efforts are enough. And you feel peace and comfort by just being in the temple. That means the temple is for you, too, and not just the people for whom you are acting as proxy.

So much of life leaves us feeling incomplete. More and more, we as humans feel disconnected from each other. But in the temple, we make eternal connections that help us feel complete. We bring whole families together in a bond that, if they choose it to be so, will never be broken. Joseph Smith refers to this binding of families as "a bold doctrine . . . a power which records or binds on earth and binds in heaven" (Doctrine and Covenants 128:9). And bold it is, for it won't be well with us "unless there is a welding link of some kind or other between fathers and children" (verse 18).

My son is a welder, and I've watched him join two pieces of metal together to create a seemingly unbreakable union. Yet this welding is nothing compared to what priesthood power can bind in the temple. To feel this bond will strengthen you and your spouse and your marriage like nothing else can. We get a taste of forever in a mortal world, and it is calming and healing. As you and your spouse attend the temple, you will take home the feeling of being completely enough. The Lord wants you to have that feeling, so please, come to His holy house.

20

Do I Do That?

In the New Testament, we read, "And why beholdest thou the mote that is in thy brother's eye, but considerest not the beam that is in thine own eye?" (Matthew 7:3). I remember when I learned the "beam" and "mote" lesson. My husband and I hadn't been married long and he did something annoying—really annoying. In fact, this annoying thing was kind of a habit and it *bugged* me. As all sorts of super judgey thoughts flew through my mind, a question came to me: *Do I do that?* The power of this question physically stopped me. I stood for a moment in the middle of our kitchen, with this question on a loop in my mind. More questions came. *Do I do annoying things regularly? Does my husband feel like this about me?*

Scenes came to my mind in a parade of unsightly things I had done—one Veruca scene after another (in case you don't know, she's the demanding, spoiled brat who, in *Willie Wonka and the Chocolate*

Factory [Warner Bros., 1971] sings "I Want It Now"). The Spirit had provided me with a trip down memory lane . . . and it was unpleasant, to say the least. I felt dizzy and wanted to go lie down in a darkened room with a cold compress on my forehead.

When I could gather myself and summon the courage, I answered the question *Do I do this?* with a resounding yes. This answer was loud, filling my brain. The answer rang in my ears and stuck to the back of my throat. I can be annoying, sometimes much more so than what now seemed a small infraction by my husband. I had judged him . . . and rather harshly.

Through all this self-discovery—and with Veruca stomping about my mind's stage—I could still hear a small voice pointing out that my husband had yet to say anything about any of this. The beam I thought would require surgery to remove from his eye, all while I made judgmental self-improvement suggestions, was really in my eye, but I couldn't see it until now.

I went through a major overhaul as I stood in the kitchen, pulling a figurative log out of my eye. But I did it and it taught me an important lesson. When my husband does something annoying and I am ready to pounce with judgment, I ask myself, *Do I do that?* The answer is usually yes, which dramatically changes what I do and say next.

Poor Veruca rarely makes an appearance anymore.

21

Mowing Lawns and Folding Jeans

I was given two interesting bits of marriage advice, one at my reception and the other just recently. An older woman, whom I had known for years, instructed me at my wedding reception, "Remember, if you never learn how to mow a lawn, no one will ever expect you to mow a lawn." Sadly, that ship had already sailed for me. I grew up mowing my family's lawn and was quite good at it, and my husband knew that. So, I chose to take this woman's advice a little differently.

We all have our areas of expertise—the things we do well—and, therefore, those tasks fall into our wheelhouse. For example, I'm good at running schedules and keeping money straight. My husband grew up on a farm and instinctively handles land, animals, and equipment like a boss. I'm good at managing the family, he's good at managing a business. But sometimes life will throw you a curve and you have to let your spouse do what you're good at. Although you are the expert at mowing the lawn, there will be times when you have to stand back and let your spouse mow it. And it might really bug you. This is where the second bit of advice comes in.

I was talking to a dear friend a few days ago. She works at a western clothing shop and was describing her recent task of folding an entire wall of jeans. She showed me a picture and, of course, it was done perfectly. She's awesome that way, as was her advice. She noticed how each store employee folds jeans differently. "Everyone folds jeans their own way, and that's okay. The same can be said about our responsibilities in marriage." I thought of the lawn-mowing advice and all the times I've had to stand back and allow my husband to help me with something I usually do. He didn't do it like I did—he didn't "fold the jeans" my way. But he was willing to help me, and that's what counts. It's what makes us partners. Sometimes I handle this graciously, sometimes not. I've learned, though, if you have to switch it up, let your spouse mow the lawn and fold the jeans his or her way, even if it doesn't get done as well as you would do it.

22

Supporting Each Other: You're My Team

When my young grandson was sick late one night, and his mom (my daughter) was helping him in the bathroom for the fourth time, he patted her on the shoulder and said with all the love and gratitude a sick four-year-old can muster, "You're my team." It brought her to tears how, with just a few words, he could sum up what it means to support each other.

Now that you're married, you and your spouse need to be each other's team. But what does that look like? Here are a few ideas.

For my grandson, who recently started team sports during that long night in the bathroom, the idea of his friends cheering for him while he kicked a ball was the ultimate expression of love and was present in his mind even when he was sick. He said the words that were in his heart. His mom was his team. The support we give each other in marriage can be the same sort of heartfelt cheering, but on a much deeper level. We can say words to our spouse that help her or him believe in herself or himself. Sometimes this isn't easy—we don't know what to say. But if we pray about it, the words will come. SAY THEM when they do.

Another way to show your spouse you're on his or her team is to suit up and show up—another favorite expression of my grandson's. Simply put, you are there to help with whatever is important to him or her. Your spouse's goals are your goals. When you do this for each other, you can accomplish anything together.

Every time I think of my grandson's statement, the ultimate marriage "team" comes to mind: Adam and Eve. How they must have supported each other while being driven from Heavenly Father's presence to the harshness of our world! It is beyond me how they did this. Yet, I try to imagine how they treated each other, how they helped and encouraged each other, and I try to pattern that in my marriage. Like my little grandson, when the going gets rough, I want my husband to know I'm his team, as I know he's mine. Go, team!

23

Put Christ at the Center

If you've had the opportunity to be sealed in the temple, then you know it is the Savior who makes this happen. He is the One who restored the sealing powers to the earth, allowing all worthy adult members of the Church to enter His home to be sealed to their families forever. To be sealed is to have the Savior's promise that even when the heavens are dust, you and your spouse can be together. This is why the Savior has to be at the center of your marriage. It won't work very well without Him.

The best way to show what this means day to day is to look at how the Savior saved each of us—through His Atonement. We wouldn't have a chance to return to Heavenly Father without Jesus Christ. We're mortal and make mistakes and need forgiveness, which He freely gives to us as we have a broken heart and a contrite spirit. We need to do the same in our marriage. We will do and say things that hurt each other. Seek forgiveness and give it as freely and completely as the Savior does. Say "I'm sorry" and "I forgive you" to your spouse—often.

When you and your husband or wife knelt across the altar in the temple, you took each other's hand in a special way, a reminder of Christ and His Atonement. This remembrance is between you and your spouse at the very moment you are sealed, and it can be there each time you forgive and offer love to each other. Christ is there at the center, where He should always be.

24

Sneak-Watching and the Vow of Trust

In today's world, people have become an impatient lot when it comes to entertainment. We can have at our fingertips an entire television series void of all commercials. During my childhood this type of luxury was something we only dreamed of. But now it's a way of life. It comes with a vow of trust, though. What friends or family members watch together, you do not sneak-watch on your own.

Growing up we had the vow of trust—it just looked different. For example, we never called our friends when certain TV shows were on. Never! And if you absolutely had to call someone, you did it during a commercial. In fact, we had to do everything during commercials—dishes, homework, feed the dog, go to the bathroom. We ran like the wind to do these things, because if you missed part of a program, you missed it. That was it. Being able to record a show or movie on a VCR tape was a mind-blowing revolution.

Now we can watch anything, anywhere, at any time. But the vow of trust is still there. I learned this the hard way, because I sneak-watched. I'm not proud to admit it, but here goes.

At the time, video rental stores were in their heyday. TV series were going to DVDs, so we could binge-watch them without commercials. For those of us who grew up being held hostage by three minutes of commercials, this kind of freedom felt like a drug. A friend of mine and my husband's recommended the crime drama *24* (FOX, 2001–10). My husband and I became addicted. Our days were full to the bursting point with a growing business and five children, yet we found ourselves staying up until the wee hours of the morning watching Kiefer Sutherland's character, Jack Bauer, save the world.

Rick and I would fly through our evenings, doing dinner and baths and bedtime faster than the speed of light. Once everything and everyone was settled, we'd get out whatever *24* season we were on and tell ourselves we were only going to watch three episodes, which would turn into four and five or more. This was a fun but exhausting escape for us . . . until the series became increasingly intense. As Jack Bauer developed into the anti-hero he became famous for, it was too much for me. I had to know what was going to happen next.

My sneak-watching indiscretion occurred somewhere in season 5. My husband was at work, all the kids were at school, and I had the house to myself. I was going to just watch for a few minutes, to find out what happened next so I could quit thinking about it. Before I knew it, I had burned through the DVD and it was time to pick the kids up from school.

Of course, I left off at a new, intense, what's-going-to-happen-next moment, because that's one of the reasons the series was so wildly popular and addictive. But I now had a much bigger problem on my hands. I had broken the vow of trust and needed to cover it up.

One of the super-annoying things I do is keep up a running monologue while Rick and I watch a show or movie. "Why is he doing that? That's stupid. Don't go in there, the ax murderer is in there." My husband kindly puts up with this and never complains. But on this particular evening, when we busted out the *24* DVD—the one I'd spent the day watching—I was uncharacteristically quiet. And Rick noticed. It could have also been the guilt plastered all over my face. I tried hard to act like I hadn't sneak-watched, but I couldn't pull it off. And when I finally admitted what I'd done, the look on my husband's face was crushing. I had broken the vow of trust.

Now, breaking the relatively harmless vow of show watching might be a funny example about trust, but there's a moral to this story. My husband and I have learned over the years that there are many parts of marriage that, when shared, *do* become sacred. And I had impatiently and selfishly experienced for myself what we had planned to experience together. It wasn't worth it. Hold sacred those together experiences and they will be even more fun and exciting when you share them. Even if you have to wait a few hours to find out how Jack will save the world this time.

25

Anniversaries and Expectations

Have you experienced a wedding anniversary yet? If not, you will . . . I hope. How will you celebrate? What, for you, will be the best way to celebrate this important day?

You may think a romantic trip is the best way to remember such a special occasion, but whether or not you can make this happen will depend on your circumstances and finances. Some years, your romantic trip may be as far as your favorite taco shop. And some years that taco shop may be in Hawaii. But the critical thing is to talk about it now. Tell each other your anniversary hopes, big and small. Let your spouse know what's on your mind. It can mean a lot to know that your loved one longs to take you to an exotic local, even if your budget can't support it yet. The best way to avoid disappointed expectations is communication. Decide together what your anniversaries will be like and then enjoy them, no matter where the tacos are made.

26

Obedience: Safety and Peace

Keep the commandments; keep the commandments!
In this there is safety; in this there is peace.
He will send blessings; he will send blessings.
Words of a prophet:
Keep the commandments.
In this there is safety and peace.

("Keep the Commandments," lyrics and music by
Barbara A. McConochie, in *Children's Songbook*
[Salt Lake City, UT: The Church of Jesus Christ of
Latter-day Saints, 1989], p. 146).

I love this Primary song. Since you are newlyweds, the likelihood
of you being called to teach a Primary class together is pretty high.

I don't know why this is the case. Perhaps it's some not-so-subtle way to encourage young couples to begin their families (though I think it may have the opposite effect). In any case, it may be good to familiarize yourselves with some popular Primary songs. "Keep the Commandments," in particular, teaches a powerful lesson that may apply to your new lives together more than you think.

"Safety" and "peace" aren't just words that make the song work. These terms speak of powerful promises for being obedient to your covenants. Through obedience you are kept safe from evils, both big and small, that can rob you of your relationship. It seems, though, that it always begins with small things. For example, does technology have too big a place in your lives? Does it connect you with your spouse, or separate the two of you? Do you do the basic but essential things like scripture study, prayer, and temple attendance? The safety that obedience will bring to your marriage is worth every effort.

Obedience also brings peace. It allows us to enter the temple, where peace prevails against the outside world. There is simplicity in the temple that enables us to see our spouse as he or she really is—not as an object to gratify our desires, but as a son or daughter of God, and as our partner in a sacred work. Obedience can bring about miracles, and what is more miraculous than safety and peace in a fallen world?

Speaking of miracles, here is a bit of advice for that inevitable Primary calling: bring treats.

27

Adulting and the Rabbit Hole of Excuses

I've always hated the term "rabbit hole." Not being a fan of confined spaces, I feel trapped at the image my mind conjures up when someone mentions a rabbit hole. Yet what better term is there to show what happens when we take a path that's not easy to leave? And it seems there are rabbit holes aplenty when we make big life decisions like getting married and beginning "adulting" together.

As married adults, you've made it through some wonderful though challenging rites of passage—dating, courtship, and planning and executing a wedding. Now it's time for some well-earned fun and relaxation. You want to spend time together and, therefore, may want to excuse yourselves from some of life's responsibilities. If you don't show up to a family function or a ward service project, we're all going to chuckle and think, "Well, they're newlyweds." If you forget to wish your sister a happy birthday or don't do your elder's quorum or Relief Society ministering, we'll shrug it off with a smile. No one will expect the adulting to happen for a while. But at some point—and you'll know when—you run the risk of falling in the rabbit hole of excuses, when being newlyweds becomes the reason to not adult.

One way to stay a safe distance from this rabbit hole is to set your priorities early on. Be dependable in your callings, remember your family and friends, and look outside yourselves for people you can lift. Of course, only you and your husband or wife can decide what your married adult life will look like. And you can always find a reason to skip your meetings and not go to the temple—in other words, to not do what will strengthen your marriage. Excuses will seem easily justified. So, right now, vow to each other that you won't go down this rabbit hole. Besides, who wants to be trapped in a dirt tunnel the size of your thigh? It would feel awful.

28

Boundaries and Threshing Out Your Own Difficulties

In a world that is constantly invading our privacy, healthy boundaries are crucial for a healthy marriage relationship. I love this quote by President Spencer W. Kimball, surprisingly from forty years ago: "Being human, you may someday have differences of opinion resulting even in little quarrels. Neither of you will be so unfaithful to the other as to go back to your parents or friends and discuss with them your little differences. That would be gross disloyalty. Your intimate life is your own and must not be shared with or confided in others. You will not go back to your people for sympathy, but will thresh out your own difficulties" (Spencer W. Kimball, *Marriage* [Salt Lake City, UT: Deseret Book Co., 1978], 25).

Before I go further, it's imperative to note that President Kimball used the word "little" TWICE to describe the differences he's speaking of. In grave matters such as broken covenants and abuse, a spouse should seek help wherever and however he or she feels safe. These are not the type of differences we are speaking of. But with "little quarrels" or "little differences," it is important to take care of them between yourself and your spouse. In fact, learning the "threshing" process will be one of the most important parts of your marriage.

An interesting word, "threshing." It brings to mind a hot, sweaty day in the field. I don't think President Kimball chose the word by chance. Threshing is the harvesting process where the edible part of the grain is separated from the husks and straw, or chaff, as it is commonly called. Perhaps President Kimball used the imagery of threshing to help us see the importance of separating ourselves from the world so that together, as husband and wife, we can harvest a solution to our differences.

With boundaries drawn to include just the two of you and the Spirit, you are left to use your own words and opinions and listen more intently to your own hearts. Without "your people," whom you may have persuaded to sympathetically choose your side, it comes down to you and your spouse to openly and tenderly discuss feelings and decide on a solution. It needs to be just the two of you out there in that field, sweating it out.

Perhaps your family and friends have used different methods of problem solving, but now, as husband and wife, you have a chance to choose your own way. Thresh it out, just the two of you. You will find that the harvest of greater love and understanding is worth some time in the field.

29

Communication and the Ultimate Normal

On many occasions, I've been told that our family is weird because we talk about our feelings . . . a lot. We get right in there and take a long, hard look at whatever emotions are traveling through the village. We don't jostle awkwardly around huge elephants in the room. We stare those suckers down, analyze them, and dissect them until they're nothing but peanut shells on the floor. This is normal for us — but it's not normal for everyone. In fact, it can make some people really uncomfortable.

As parents, it's both fascinating and frightening when you realize your children consider you the ultimate normal. For years, my husband owned and operated a restoration company, so my children thought all dads cleaned up after floods and fires. I did a great deal of sewing when my children were young, so they thought all moms made prom dresses for everyone. Of course, mothers and fathers do all sorts of different things. Some fathers are doctors and make a truckload of money. And some moms are smart and just *buy* prom dresses. Some moms even have the UPS man deliver them. But just like my family's elephant-devouring communication patterns, whatever it is you do will be *your* family's ultimate normal. No pressure. But here are a few things to think about.

When two people marry, they bring together two definitions of normal. It would be a good idea for you and your spouse to define exactly what your "normal"s are, especially when it comes to communication. Write them down, even (there are some note pages at the end of this book . . . just sayin'). Is it effortless for you to talk about your feelings, while your spouse may need some time and space to feel safe enough to do so? You may think you know this about each other from the time you spent dating. You don't. So, look closely at your "normal"s and talk about them, and then decide what will be normal for your relationship. And then someday your children will go out into the world with the definition of normal you've given them, and people will look at them like they're complete weirdos. It's the cycle of life.

30

Keeping Score Is for Basketball, Not Marriage

Perhaps you've seen them—couples who walk around with imaginary scoreboards above their heads, complete with flashing lights and numbers so large everyone can see them. A spouse like this knows exactly how many times his or her spouse has messed up—he or she is keeping score and means business. And those flashing numbers don't let anyone forget anything.

If you're in the National Basketball Association, this is great. An enormous amount of time, effort, and money is spent keeping track of every move made by every player on the court. Good and bad, each player is analyzed and re-analyzed to consider his worth on the team. And these stats go back for decades. This sort of thing is not so good in marriage. In fact, it can be a seriously bad thing, because along with scorekeeping we find "the closet," where the supposedly forgotten mistakes are quietly waiting in the dark to be dragged out and thrust in someone's face, over and over again. It is a harsh road that leads a couple to closets and scorekeeping because there's no true forgiveness between them.

It's human to want to keep track of our hurts. Like little children showing off their scars from battle wounds, we want other people—especially the ones who caused the wounds in the first place—to be reminded of every gash. But the only person who is ever justified in doing this is the Savior, and thankfully, He doesn't. His love and mercy are beyond our comprehension. And when He forgets, He forgets forever. It's His wounds that allow us to be free from all pain and to truly heal. It is His example, not the NBA's, that we need to follow in our marriage relationship.

So, if you see yourself and your spouse heading toward scoreboards and closets, do the smart thing—take a sledgehammer and obliterate those closets and scoreboards. Then remind yourselves that we all fall short and mess up. We all need forgiveness . . . true forgiveness. No closets. No scores.

31

Habit-Forming on Steroids

"Depending on what they are, our habits will either make us or break us. We become what we repeatedly do" (Sean Covey, *The 7 Habits of Highly Effective Teens* [New York: Simon and Schuster, 2014], 8). Mr. Covey's statement, though directed toward teens, applies to us all. But I believe his point is given a dose of steroids when applied to marriage because of what happens when we live with someone.

It's a major life change to live together. You share the same space—and the same feeling in that space. You and your spouse can't help but cue off each other, which greatly affects what you repeatedly do each day. For example, if my husband is reading, I'll usually pick up a book and sit next to him and read. If I'm working in the garden, he'll come out and help me. And almost always, if one of us is eating, the other will join in, usually eating the very same thing.

We have our own daily tasks, but what we do in our relaxed time together is strongly influenced by each other. As you can see and may have already found out in your own marriage, the ability to form habits as a couple is greater than the ability to form habits as a single or alone person.

Over the years my husband and I developed some bad habits. We've succeeded in replacing some of these with better habits, but some (like eating ice cream straight from the carton while lying in bed watching TV) we've given up trying to change and have embraced as part of our lifestyle. But we've also worked at forming some good habits—little things we try to do every day—like pray together, talk about our feelings for the Savior, and be kind. It never ceases to amaze me how much easier it is to form these habits together as a married couple than for one person to try to form these habits all alone.

What habits will you form as a couple? What will you repeatedly do that will cue your spouse? Whom will you become, together and on your own? However you choose to answer these questions, keep in mind that Heavenly Father has given you a great dose of steroids to help you—living with your spouse.

32

Birthday Baggage: Blame Your Mom

What were birthdays like for you growing up? Was this special day marked with a well-wish and your favorite dinner, or a blowout at the local theme park, with candy and tokens flowing freely? Did your dad construct a slip 'n' slide out of a giant roll of plastic and dish soap for you and your friends, or was it more of a formal affair with aunts and uncles and smartly wrapped gifts? Did you pummel a piñata? Perhaps your mom baked you a birthday cake and, regardless your age, decorated it with a ridiculous amount of icing and sprinkles? (This was my particular sin.) Whatever made up the birthdays of your youth, it's just the two of you now, you and your spouse . . . and all your birthday baggage.

From this point on, the mothers take a back seat with the birthday gigs, and the spouse is on point. This can be a little stressful. We can't help but come to marriage with our own birthday expectations.

Does your husband or wife know that for as long as you can remember you've had a green pancake in the shape of your name for your birthday breakfast? There's only one way to eliminate this kind of stress, and that's to talk about it. Let each other know what says "birthday" to you. True, your mom just always knew. But to be perfectly honest, mothers are making this up as they go. So, decide with your spouse how you'll celebrate your birthdays. And as you load up her or his birthday cake with five pounds of icing and sprinkles, you can blame the moms.

33

Scripture Study:
Wear Stretchy Pants and Feast

One of my seminary teachers always referred to scripture study as "feasting on the word of God." It's a familiar analogy used in the scriptures, but this teacher took it a step further, drawing elaborate parallels between the scriptures and scrumptious foods. I'm a gal who enjoys her food, but I never experienced this connection with the scriptures. He would describe elaborate buffets with juicy meats, creamy potato dishes, fluffy bread, and rich desserts—the ultimate food fantasy. This seminary class was right before lunch, so it was a particularly effective teaching strategy. Yet I was an adult before I felt the scriptures fill me physically, emotionally, and spiritually as if I'd been to a literal feast. But when it clicked it really clicked. Wanting this feast daily, I happily showed up in my spiritual stretchy pants.

Your schedule will be different now that you're married, but don't let your personal scripture feast get bumped. Equally as important, set aside some time to feast on the scriptures with your husband or wife. It will do amazing things for your relationship. Stopping everything else for a while and focusing on the Lord will help create the bond that comes when you and your spouse learn together. You can reset your mind and see things as they really are. You can testify to each other. You can remember the plan of salvation and why you are here on earth. These are just a few examples, but whatever you experience will help you do what you do better because it will connect you with the love of God. It will fill you like nothing else can. So, put on your spiritual stretchy pants, pull up two chairs, and dig into the feast. It will only do you good.

34

Counsel Together . . . or in Other Words, Negotiate Nicely

Life boils down to making decisions. We make dozens, big and small, every day. Now that you're married, though, you need to make the big decisions together. And perhaps several of the small ones, too. How are you at decision-making? Are you quick or does it take you a while? Once you make a decision, do you second-guess yourself? Do you buy something and then end up taking it back, only to go buy it again? How are you with paint colors and ordering food in restaurants? Decision-making is a skill you bring to your marriage, and it's best to know where each of you stand at it.

You'll probably get hit with some big decisions right off the bat. Where to live, where to go to school, where to work, student loans, vehicles (do you need two or can you get by with one?), etc. The list of decisions can be lengthy, and I'm sure you and your spouse each have opinions about them all—including some rather strong opinions.

You may be used to making these big decisions on your own, but now you have a spouse to consider. Some may refer to this as counseling together, but I like to call it "negotiating nicely."

Negotiating nicely may look like different things to different people. I think the best place to start is what it *doesn't* look like. There is no manipulation and coercion. No one tries to overpower the other spouse. There is no disrespect, and certainly no anger or mean words. Negotiating nicely is trying to see the other person's perspective and understand why that person wants what he or she wants. And this isn't always easy. Each of us will feel we have the best solution, and our spouse needs to understand this. But hear each other out and, most importantly, be nice about it. Because when you're nice, the Holy Ghost can be with you. He will inspire and direct you both to the right decision. This is what you want. So, don't just negotiate—negotiate nicely.

35

Intimacy

I've heard so many definitions for the word "intimacy." I'm going to try to give it one that will do justice to this powerful part of marriage. Intimacy is communication in all its forms. From a glance and a touch, to open conversation, to passionate love, it's what unites husband and wife. The key, though, is safety. Do you feel safe enough with your spouse to be completely open—about everything?

You probably haven't been married for long and may feel you are as open and safe as your time together has allowed. But over the years, life will give you new circumstances, not all pleasant and conducive to easy communication. Your intimacy needs to grow and adjust along with the demands of life. How, though? Here are some ideas.

Try to be flexible. This has been a hard lesson for me to learn, but an invaluable one. My husband was a widower when we married. He had three young children, whom I've loved as if they came from me. Eventually, we added two more children. My husband's parents have lived with us since we got married. They are dear to us and have brought many blessings into our lives. So, when it came to privacy, my husband and I had to learn early on to be flexible. We had to give up what we thought newlywed life should look like, and embrace our circumstances as they were. When we did this we grew closer, and our communication became more open and safe. We changed our expectations and treasured our private moments together.

Have a sense of humor. I've always felt that if you can laugh at it, you can deal with it. And you'd be amazed at what you can laugh at. As you can imagine, privacy was a hot commodity at our house. Living in a very small home with three children and my husband's parents, Rick and I had many failed attempts at a few quiet moments together. We learned to laugh at this. . . and at ourselves.

Something else to think about. Heavenly Father *wants* us to have open and safe communication. Passion is a feeling He gave us, yet the world associates sex with empty objectification. Those of us who grew up in the Church have been taught since our youth to bridle our sexual feelings. Some of these teachings, usually from well-meaning parents, have carried the unspoken message that sexual feelings are bad—that you're not a good person if you have these feelings. Then, after a five-minute ceremony, they are no longer bad, but good and expected. Some people can't switch mental gears this quickly. We need to remember that sexuality is a gift from God and that He wants us—within the bonds of marriage—to find joy in these feelings.

In fact, this marital relationship is the key to happiness. President Boyd K. Packer declared in general conference: "The commandment to multiply and replenish the earth has never been rescinded. It is essential to the plan of redemption and is the source of human happiness. Through the righteous exercise of this power, we may come close to our Father in Heaven and experience a fulness of joy, even godhood. The power of procreation is not an incidental part of the plan; it is the plan of happiness; it is the key to happiness. The desire to mate in humankind is constant and very strong. Our happiness in mortal life, our joy and exaltation are dependent upon how we respond to these persistent, compelling physical desires" (Boyd K. Packer, "The Plan of Happiness," *Ensign*, May 2015).

How will you and your spouse respond to these desires throughout your life together? How will your intimacy grow and strengthen throughout mortality's changing seasons? How will your communication become closer and safer? Seek Heavenly Father's guidance for the answers to these questions. I promise He will tell you what is right for your relationship, because He wants both of you to be happy—together. As President Packer said so perfectly in that same talk, "The end of all activity in the Church is to see that a man and a woman with their children are happy at home, sealed for eternity."

36

Traditions: Why Are We Doing This?

We all like the idea of traditions. For children, they can be a grounding and stabilizing part of family life, and at the same time fill us with tummy-twirling anticipation. Christmas, Thanksgiving, Easter, for example, are all chock-full of opportunities for family traditions. Does everyone sit around watching Mom wrestle the lights on the Christmas tree, then join in the fun of hanging the ornaments? Is saying one thing you're thankful for the price you pay for a turkey drumstick on Thanksgiving? Do you hide chocolate Easter eggs in your yard even though you live where the average temperature on that day is 100°F? My personal favorite is giving each other slightly weird Christmas pajamas on Christmas Eve, though I don't know how much my children enjoy this particular tradition. There was that one unfortunate sleep-sack year.

What traditions will you and your spouse begin? Will you continue the traditions from your families, or create your own? Something to keep in mind is that traditions usually require planning and work. There needs to be some meaning behind them so when life gets crazy, you'll still go to the effort. The meaning can be of a personal nature, or to simply have fun together. Or it can be the selfish delight of watching your new son-in-law try to impress you by wearing the ridiculous red sleep sack you gave him on Christmas Eve. Whatever the purpose of your traditions, teach them to your children. Explain to them why you're doing what you're doing, and your traditions will become part of your family's foundation.

37

Grooming—Do It for You and Yours

I am fifty-five years old. Please keep that in mind when I say I get ready *almost* every day. In other words, I do my hair, apply some makeup, and wear a clean outfit that might even have been ironed. I was raised in a time where you just did this. You didn't think of leaving the house not ready for the day. Even if you weren't going anywhere, what if someone came by? My friends and I took blow dryers and hot rollers to girls' camp. The poor groundskeeper never had a moment's rest because we constantly blew out the electrical circuits.

Looking back, I don't completely agree with the image thing that went on back then. But developing the habit of getting ready every day has taught me a few things about myself. I feel good when I'm groomed. Not because I always have to be in full makeup and hair to be a worthwhile person, but because I feel good and strong when I try to look my best. It's called self-respect. When I feel good about myself, I'm ready to take on the day and greet the people I cross paths with—neighbors, friends, the grocery-store clerk, the UPS man, the drive-through server from whom I purchase my daily dose of carbonated diet soda, and, especially, my spouse and family.

That leads me to something else I've learned from years of firing up my hot rollers. Now that you're married, you represent other people, especially your spouse. You're the face of your family—when people see you, they see your spouse and your children. How will you do that? I can tell you how *not* to do it. It's known in my home as The Day Mom Chose Not to Groom. It was a Saturday morning and I decided to not care—I wasn't going to get ready for the day. I lasted until about noon, when I got tired of my kids asking if I was sick. And frankly, I felt grimy. I showered and had just finished putting rollers in my hair, when there was a commotion at the front of our house. I stepped around the corner and found my front room filled with my husband's mission president, several mission companions, and their wives—who, by the way, all looked great. They had decided to surprise us with an impromptu reunion. And there I stood in all my glory, wearing my pajamas and rollers at noon. Yes, it was a Saturday and they had surprised us and taken their chances as to what state they would catch us in. But these were important people to my husband, and I wanted to look better than I did. Once my children figured out I wasn't sick and that all of this was just a failed attempt at grooming rebellion, they laughed their heads off. They still laugh about it.

Now, there are always going to be days when the grooming just doesn't happen—illness, babies, emergencies. But on the whole, you'll feel better if you're clean and have clean clothes on . . . especially if somebody's mission president pops in. Most importantly, though, do it for yourself and for those you represent, out of respect and love.

38

In That Very Moment

For my entire life, I've lived on the same block and in the same ward. When my husband and I got married, we moved around the corner from where I grew up. This unique experience has allowed me to know and associate with the same people—some of the best people I know—for forever. One such couple were like second parents to me. During my childhood, their home was a haven, and after I grew up, it was a place where I could seek advice and encouragement. Many times, I sat at their kitchen table and shared whatever they were having for lunch . . . and listened to them. I learned so much from this wonderful pair. Their love was palpable. It drew you in, encircled you, and held you in an embrace you didn't want to leave. Being with them, in their home, was like being in the temple.

Not long before he passed away, I asked this wonderful man what the key was to a happy marriage. He answered, "Don't do anything that will cause the Spirit to withdraw from you." He told me of an exchange between him and his wife just a few days before. He had said something short and impatient to her and then left the room. At once he felt the Spirit withdraw from him. That felt awful, as it always does, and in that very moment he sought his wife's forgiveness. "Don't let even the smallest conflict go unattended," he told me. "Little things have a way of stacking up until they seem overwhelming to deal with. Take care of them early on so you always have the Spirit with you."

That is wise counsel for us all.

39

Communication—Just Listen or the Quick Fix

We humans have a tendency to fall into two communication camps—Just Listen or The Quick Fix. When we have a problem, some of us want to talk about it, hash it out, whine a little. And some of us want to fix it quickly and move on. To be somewhere in the middle of these two would be a good thing, but many times we aren't. So, it may be wise for you and your spouse to look closely at these two camps and talk about where each of you stand, because you'll need to fix a lot of problems together.

Listeners are emotional about their problem. They want to talk about it and have someone sincerely listen to them. They don't necessarily want someone to fix the problem, which on the outside may make absolutely no sense. But in the mind of the listener it does, because what she or he really needs is to be understood. The listener knows how to fix the problem, but just doesn't want to be alone in the fixing. It's complicated. The important thing to remember is that listeners need to be listened to no matter how unproductive it may seem. And this is precisely what drives fixers nuts.

Fixers take the emotions out of the problem—take it down to its bare bones and fix the darn thing. And they like to do it fast, in five minutes or less. Talking about it is nonproductive, listening even more so. It's all about fixing the problem so we all can move on to something better.

So, what if one of you is a listener and one of you is a fixer? It can truly feel like you're sitting in two completely different camps. And it can feel lonely. Thankfully, we are shown how to deal with this. The story of Jesus raising Lazarus from the dead is one of my favorites. Lazarus's death was an opportunity for Jesus to teach those around Him. It was a problem He could fix. And yet He took time to listen to Mary and Martha, grieve with them, and even weep with them before He brought Lazarus back. Jesus showed compassion and patience with His good friends as they struggled with their problem, even though He knew He could quickly fix it, which He did. The Savior was clearly in both camps. There are many examples where He was in one camp or the other, but regardless, He showed nothing but love.

We need to try to do the same. Whichever camp we're in—whether we're listeners or fixers—we need to try to have compassion and patience for each other. We can try to understand someone's need for a listening ear and try to see the wisdom in a possible solution offered by a fixer. It will make fixing problems together so much easier.

40

Holidays and Ground Rules

Your first holiday season with your spouse will be a special time filled with memories you'll cherish. It may also be the first holiday since you moved out of your parents' house. They and the rest of your family will want you and your new husband or wife to celebrate with them. Be patient with your family. This is a big change. Here are a few ideas that might help everybody stay in the holiday spirit.

You may have many invitations from both sides of the family. It's not going to be easy to tell your mom you can't be there for the traditional Christmas-morning brunch because you'll be brunching it up with your spouse's family. You can try to squeeze everybody in, racing from one family meal to another. But do you really want to show up, with eyes bulging, to your fourth dinner on Thanksgiving Day, seriously regretting not wearing some form of Spandex? I've seen this and it's not fun or pretty.

It might be wise to lay some ground rules right from the start. You can switch it up each year—one family one year, the other family the next. Or spend Christmas Eve with one family, Christmas Day with the other. Perhaps you can do something special with extended family the day before or the day after—help with baking the day before Thanksgiving, or go on an after-Christmas shopping trip. Talk about it as spouses and decide on a plan that will work for both of you.

Whichever way you decided to divvy up your love among the family, be sure to save some time for just the two of you. You're a family unit now, so stake your claim and have some fun. It might take a few seasons to adjust, though, so keep the Spandex handy.

41

Order Calms

Life as newlyweds can be crazy busy. You may be in school, one of you is probably working, and if we toss in a few Church callings and the responsibility of making a home together, your life can be nuts. But there are a few things you and your spouse can do to avoid feeling overwhelmed.

I have two words beautifully calligraphed and framed on the wall of my kitchen: "Order Calms." It's simple—order helps us stay in control of our lives, and that is always calming. I've tried to live by these words. But how do you translate them into your crazy-busy days? One way is to try to do a few things at the same time each day. Go to bed at a decent hour that allows you to get consistent sleep. Get out of bed at around the same time every day. Make your bed. Eat meals at normal times. Sit down at a table with your spouse and take a few moments to reconnect, even if it's over a bowl of cold cereal.

Pray and study regularly. Doing these simple tasks together each day will add a solid sense of order, help you feel in control, and go a long way toward relieving stress.

Another way to add order to your lives is to keep up on the not-fun stuff. Organize your bills and finances so they are easy for both of you to do. Keep on top of your emails and your regular mail. Sync your calendar with your spouse's so you know each other's schedules and don't miss important appointments. Put things away. Keep a running grocery list on your refrigerator or phone and add to it as you run low on items. This may seem like overkill for just the two of you, since you think you'll remember everything you need once you get to the store. But I guarantee you won't remember. In fact, without a list, you'll go over your budget and will walk out of the store without the important items you went there for. Make grocery lists a part of your lives. Nothing can add stress to your day like running out of toilet paper.

This world is becoming increasingly stressful, which is why the peace and calmness of the temple is such a dramatic contrast to our lives. There are many reasons we feel removed from the world when we enter the Lord's house, one being that it is a house of order. There's a schedule in the temple. Records are kept. It's tidy. You know what to expect. Although we can't have everything perfectly ordered like this, we can try to pattern our lives and homes after the temple. It will bring calmness and great blessings in a crazy world.

42

Keep Something in the Trough

"Keep something in the trough" is a strange expression, yet good imagery when describing self-care. Some people like to compare emotional reserves to a well of water, and I guess that works. But a well receives its water from an underground source we rarely see, so the water seems to magically appear. Since emotional reserves don't just magically appear, I prefer the image of a trough. Anyone who has ever filled a trough with water—maybe with a bucket—knows there's nothing magical about it. Filling a trough takes effort, just like keeping an emotional reserve takes effort.

If you've ever experienced that moment when your very last emotional drop has drained away, you'll know what I mean when I say it isn't an easy moment. But it can happen if we're not careful. How do you keep some water in your trough, especially with the demands of a new life with your spouse? A good place to start is to talk about what it is that replenishes your emotional reserve, and what replenishes the emotional reserves of your husband or wife. Is it solitude or connecting with a group of friends? Is it reading, watching a movie, or going for a long run? It could be very different things for each of you, and that's okay. Whatever it is, make sure your spouse knows what you need.

Knowing what fills each other's troughs can be a tremendous blessing and strength to your marriage. It's a real partner that watches for signs of emotional drought and then does what it takes to enable the other person to fill up. Maybe it's arranging for some quiet time, or gathering friends for an evening—whatever you or your spouse needs. Be unselfish and remember that the source of your spouse's emotional replenishing may not be you. But if you know where the replenishing comes from, you can make it happen.

There are so many things in life that can drain a person's emotional trough. Often it can be hard to maintain just an inch of water. But an inch is better than empty, even if that inch is drained and replaced daily. Watch yourself and your spouse. Keep something in your troughs and stay emotionally healthy. Anything is better than empty.

43

There's Always Disneyland

Vacations are a big deal. They cost money, require time off from school and work, and take a good amount of planning. We look forward to vacations because they give us a chance to get away from responsibility and have some fun—almost like a light at the end of life's tunnel. And now that you're married, you get to vacation with your spouse. But your definition of a vacation may be completely different from her or his definition. Your vacation perspective depends on the vacations of your childhood.

What were your family vacations like? Did you take cross-country road trips visiting historical sights, learning a bunch of cool stuff and loving it? Or did you hate it and swear that when you could plan your own vacation it wouldn't involve a bronze plaque explaining the inner workings of a nineteenth-century bathroom. Was every minute of each vacation planned, with every day jam-packed to the limit, or did you have hours of free time to do as you please? What made it feel like a vacation? And what made it feel like forced family fun? Before you plan a vacation with your new spouse, talk about your definitions of a vacation. Be open and honest, and if worse comes to worse, blame your parents for your vacation perspective. We're fine with this.

One thing we can all agree on is the vacation middle-ground—Disneyland. Nothing says vacation like riding some rides, eating some churros, and buying a weird hat. You can always go there and be happy.

44

A Calling that Lasts Forever

"Husbands and wives should understand that their first calling—from which they will never be released—is to one another and then to their children" (Boyd K. Packer, "And a Little Child Shall Lead Them," *Ensign*, May 2012). As members of the Church, we are programed to know that callings come and go. Once we receive one, we usually hold it for a few years. Some callings are longer, but come with the assurance that we will eventually be released. Except when it comes to the calling of husband and wife. President Packer's quote puts the responsibilities of marriage and parenting in a clear order. And these callings are forever.

When we receive a new Church calling, we usually take some time to familiarize ourselves with what will be expected of us. We may do some reading, study what it says in the Church handbook, and indulge ourselves by purchasing a new notebook. These tasks may seem unromantic and even geeky when applied to the calling of husband and wife, yet they show that you care enough about your new calling to make it a priority and want to do well at it. If your first calling is to one another—and lasts forever—then what can you do to understand it? (Hey, you're reading this book and that's great! Way to go.)

If you truly look at your new role as husband or wife as a calling, then it is a position you can grow in. With most callings in the Church, we don't know much at first—we have to learn our way around. The same is true for the calling of husband and wife, yet we may feel we are supposed to know everything as soon as we receive the title. It is an ever-learning process, so read some other books, take some classes, talk to people you trust, and gain as much knowledge as you can about your new callings. If you are called to be Young Women president, it may take you two years to learn the program. If you're called to teach the Sunbeam class, it may take eighteen months to figure out how to get the children through Sharing Time without at least one meltdown. You will be released from these callings—aren't you grateful?—and given new ones. But your calling to be a wife or a husband will be forever. Treat it like that.

45

Gratitude in Our Daily Lives

Someone has said, "In our daily lives, we must see that it is not happiness that makes us grateful, but the gratefulness that makes us happy." For years I've searched unsuccessfully for the author of this quote so I could give credit where credit is due. In one simple sentence, this wise person reminds us of a mind-set so powerful it can change our lives. The mind-set is gratitude, and it can shape your marriage into a happy relationship, regardless of your circumstances.

Gratitude must come first. We can't be grateful only when life is great. If we're going to have gratefulness in our daily lives, we must not focus on what we don't have and think we should have. Rather, we must focus on what we *do* have—and believe it to be enough. The world, particularly social media, doesn't make this easy. If we allow it, we can be bombarded hourly by shiny, fancy, luxurious things other people own. "They're going on another trip?" "Well, that lunch had to cost fifty bucks." "Does she really need another pair of shoes?" After a while this can be the dialogue playing in an endless loop in your mind. And it's only a few short steps until you believe you need all these trips and lunches and shoes to be happy. This type of attitude can be a cancer to your marriage.

There's something almost magical about seeing what you have and believing it is enough. I understand that it's easy for me to write these words, but not so easy to apply them. Some couples start out with new homes, new cars, and exotic trips. And some much less. If you focus on someone else's things, yours will never be enough. Try instead to express your gratitude for what you do have. Verbalize this gratitude to your spouse. Every day, with your spouse, thank your Heavenly Father for the blessings He has given you. If you allow gratefulness to take a firm hold in your hearts, you will experience happiness every day.

46

"Our Main Concern Was for Each Other"

A young couple who have been happily married for over fifteen years shared an experience with me and gave me permission to include it in this book. They had been married for only a few years, he was in the most demanding year of medical school, and she had just given birth to their first child. The husband was up well before dawn to study, put in a full day of classes and clinicals, then study late into the night. It was a cold winter, and the wife spent her days with their infant daughter in their very small student apartment. The couple was active in their student ward and had made several friends, but were states away from both families and all that was familiar.

This was a trying time—what could be considered one of the hardest circumstances for a young couple. Yet, both husband and wife referred to it as one of the happiest times in their marriage. When I asked them why, they both said it was because their main focus was each other. She knew he was under a tremendous amount of pressure and trying to keep to a grueling schedule, so she'd try to find ways to ease his burden. She would think about him during the day and pray for him, asking Heavenly Father to help him. The young man knew his wife spent longs days cooped up with a baby, so he tried to find ways, even if they were small, to give her a break.

This pair could have easily been consumed in self-pity during this time, yet that wasn't the case because their focus was each other's comfort and happiness. As this couple took an unselfish approach to a difficult trial, the Lord blessed and increased and strengthened their love. The young woman and her husband were able to bear up under their burdens and see their work as a sweet labor. This hard time became a happy memory . . . and a wonderful example for us all.

47

Pedestals

We put people we love on pedestals. Sometimes we just can't help ourselves. Their glowing qualities outshine all else, and before we know it they are exalted onto a gleaming pedestal alongside the gods. But what happens when *you* are hoisted up on one of these pillars of white marble and the inevitable happens—you act human?

It feels good to be placed on a pedestal. The eyes that look up at you are filled with adoration on the brink of worship. But standing on a pedestal can be exhausting. There's not a lot of surface area up there, so it can feel cramped. After a while, you're going to want to sit down, maybe dangle your feet around . . . lie down, even. You might have a hankering for your favorite snack of chips and salsa and accidentally dribble salsa on the pristine white stone. And you may tip over your soda, because that's what humans do. The last thing we want, though, is to disappoint that adoring person gazing up at us.

It's hard to have others—especially your spouse—see your flaws. The desire to be seen as perfect is powerful. But no one can be a partner to a one-dimensional, perfect person. In the real world, pedestals always topple and crumble and make a mess that needs to be cleaned up. It might be easier to just avoid pedestals altogether. In other words, talk to your spouse about your flaws. Be willing to confront your weaknesses. You won't think less of each other—quite the opposite. Your admiration will flourish and will be grounded in reality. You will understand yourself and each other better. And nothing feels as good as being loved for who you really are.

48

Three Little Words and What They Really Mean

No, I'm not talking about "I love you." We know what those words mean. I'm talking about three other little words that, when used in certain contexts, will not mean anything close to what you think. The words are "nothing," "fine," and "whatever."

If you notice something different about your wife's behavior, like she's quiet or muttering unintelligible phrases under her breath, or forcefully closing doors and cupboards, you will probably ask her if something's wrong. If her answer is "nothing," do NOT believe her. Something is most definitely wrong. How you proceed from here will be up to your discretion—but tread carefully, for you're on dangerous ground.

"Fine" is one of those loaded, packed, bulging words that doesn't necessarily mean anything remotely close to "okay" or "all right" or "good." You can gain some clues in how it's said. If your wife says it under her breath like a whisper, then you should push to know more. But if she spits it out with extra air, you should probably stand still and be very quiet. If she almost screams it while slamming a drawer, you need to scamper on out and buy her some chocolate because she is absolutely *not* fine.

If you've tried to get to the real meaning of her "nothing" and "fine" and she answered you with the word "whatever," then you are in serious trouble. "Whatever" is in a whole different category than those other two little words. "Whatever" is a code-red emergency, and there is no mystery as to what she means by it. I could tell you the meaning, but it would be considered inappropriate and my editor would edit it out. Just start apologizing to your wife and don't quit until she stops rolling her eyes.

The English language is complicated enough without us coming along and doing what we've done with "nothing," "fine," and "whatever." Hopefully my advice will help. But if you find yourself in the maze of these three words, just remember that chocolate will usually work to help get you out. And Target gift cards. Big ones.

49

Charge Your Soul

We have become a phone-charging people. We religiously plug our phones into their chargers every night. We watch the percentage of battery life, and we panic if it gets low. We will ask complete strangers if we can borrow their chargers, and we scour stores and restaurants for charging ports. We monitor how we use our phones to conserve battery life. And nothing will start our day off poorly like having forgotten to charge our phones the night before. But do we do the same with our souls? Do we give our connection with our Heavenly Father the same hyperattentive care we give our cellular devices?

I grew up having a rotary dial phone with a three-foot cord. Our one phone was on a counter in our living room, so if you had a phone conversation, the entire house took part in your half. The phone didn't move, so you didn't move. Dating with this setup was as you would imagine it to be. On the other hand, listening to my mom's half of conversations with her Relief Society friends was very enlightening—I learned a great deal about our ward that way. Drawing upon this childhood experience, I was one of the first women in our neighborhood to purchase a cordless telephone. I had five children at home and had just been called as Relief Society president. Having privacy while talking on the phone was akin to a spiritual experience.

Your generation will know nothing but the convenience of cell phones. You have the privacy of texting, even in a crowd. You can connect with almost anyone anywhere if your phone is charged. You can also have spiritually charged souls, because Heavenly Father has made it easier than ever to connect with Him. At a touch of a finger we can enjoy scriptures and general conference talks. More and more temples are being built, and it takes only minimal effort to find the names of ancestors who need their work done. We can always pray— anywhere at any time. It's like Heavenly Father has put soul-charging ports everywhere.

What will you and your spouse do to stay charged? Will you make your souls a priority, just as you do your phones and other devices? Talk about it with your husband or wife and make a plan. Don't let the most important battery you have—your soul—run low.

50

Woo Each Other

Okay, I get that the verb "woo," as in "to woo someone," is primarily used in Regency romance novels and the random corny joke. But one definition of "woo" is "to invite by one's own action" (dictionary.com). Doesn't that create a lovely visual? As opposed to "keep dating each other," which sounds exclusively for Saturday nights, and "keep the courtship alive," which leaves an aftertaste of desperation, *wooing* someone has a cheerful, 24/7 feel to it. This is what we want.

In the context of wooing, to invite implies to ask someone to be a part of what you're doing. It could mean a Saturday-night date, but it could also mean so much more. You want your spouse to be with you, and by your actions you will make whatever you are doing together delightful and enjoyable. You are seeking the pleasure of her or his company. This can mean dinner and a movie, or grocery shopping, or washing the car, or my husband's personal favorite—

a trip to the building-supply store. As I wrote these words, I felt the women of the world wince. Yet if your spouse has an attitude of wooing, this sort of thing can be quite fun. My husband needs to get a few things and wants me to be with him. He's pleasant and funny. He appreciates my opinion and wants me to choose colors and styles. He carries everything, even my purse when it bothers my shoulder, which it often does because it's so ridiculously heavy. The point is, I don't *have* to be there. He knows all the building-supply stores like the back of his hand and can do just fine on his own. But because he invites me to go with him and through his actions shows me that he genuinely wants me there, I feel wooed.

Say what you will, but this silly-sounding word is an action word that works even after thirty-one years of marriage. To woo someone can be formal or informal, scheduled or spontaneous, but most importantly, it describes an ever-present attitude backed by deeds. So, pull "woo" out of the forgotten word pile, brush it off, and see what it can do for you. Who knew shopping for paint could be so fun?

51

Newlyweds . . . Again

Perhaps this isn't the first time you've been a newlywed. I mentioned earlier that my husband was a widower with three children when we married. It was my first marriage and his second, creating two very different perspectives to our newlywed experience. There were times it wasn't easy. It takes an unselfish heart to do this and make it work. A few things that helped us may help you.

First, remember no matter what your circumstances are, you deserve the title of newlyweds again. I will forever be grateful for my husband's approach to our unique situation. He viewed us as newlyweds in every sense of the word, since we were truly new to this life together. Because of this, I was never made to feel inadequate, even though there was much I needed to learn on the job, stepping into a ready-made family. And almost nine months to the day after we were sealed in the Mesa Arizona Temple, I gave birth to our daughter.

That first year of marriage was a humdinger! Never, though, did my husband lay out his past experience with marriage and parenting as the road map for me to follow. Rather, we talked and made decisions together, because this was all new to the both of us.

Second, you and your spouse need to create a history together, and that takes time. No matter how positively you view your new life together, your past history will always be there and can be intimidating. Be patient and give your new life the time it needs to feel like you have a history together. This was particularly hard for me. I had stepped into the middle of a growing family, surrounded by the solidness of twelve years of life I hadn't experienced. But with each vacation, Christmas, and birthday party, that history grew until it became a past that felt like my husband's and mine.

So, if you are newlyweds again, please feel worthy of the title. Wear it like a badge of honor, and see your new lives together through new eyes. Then give it some time, letting history build itself into something uniquely yours.

52

Step-Parenting and Love

"Children at once accept joy and happiness with quick familiarity, being themselves naturally all happiness and joy" (Victor Hugo, *Les Misérables* [New York City: Dodd, Mead and Company, 1862], 161). We underestimate children. They can handle much more than we think they can. This is particularly true of the spirits coming to the earth now. My husband and his first wife didn't underestimate their children. Knowing that death was inevitable, they taught their children about death from the perspective of the plan of salvation, a plan filled with joy and happiness. When they lost their beloved mother, these amazing children understood where she was, whom she was with, and what she was doing. They were quick to find comfort in their Heavenly Father's plan. It was familiar to them. Their faith was astounding, and they handled their loss with grace and confidence unmatched by most adults.

It goes without saying that being a stepparent isn't an easy role. However, I believe that Victor Hugo was onto something that will help us. Children are familiar with love. When their worlds have been turned upside down by loss or change, they quickly turn to that which is familiar. I've seen it with my children. As a stepparent, you can be that steady, safe, familiar source of love. And you can teach the children about a plan filled with joy and happiness, one that is familiar to their souls. I didn't come into step-parenting with this insight, but quickly learned it. If I can offer you one bit of advice in this area, it's this: love your children. While they are with you, love them as if they came from you. And no matter how challenging this new role may be, you will have what it takes. You will be enough.

53

Taking Down the Barriers

One afternoon as I came down the hill by my home, I was surprised to find the road closed off by a police barricade. Several police cars, a long police van, and many crowd-control barriers were blocking the road and sidewalks. There was "Caution" tape everywhere. Policemen were directing drivers to turn around—no one was getting through. As I slowly turned my vehicle around to go back the way I had come, I scanned the scene for any clue as to why this barricade was up. There was nothing. So, of course, my imagination took over and concocted all sorts of scenarios, not the least of which involved an ax murderer wielding his way through my neighborhood. (Yes, I have issues.)

The same mental sequence of events can play out in our mind when our spouse puts up an emotion barrier. We are surprised, and we have to back up, turn around, and look for clues that tell us why.

Most of all, we are frightened because we don't know what's on the other side of the barrier. That fear is difficult to deal with in a marriage.

It's a risk to allow your spouse to see a place you've kept blocked off. To be vulnerable is to hope to be able to withstand what someone will think of you, and usually we imagine the worst—judgment and ridicule. But being vulnerable also provides an opportunity for someone to love all the parts of you, even the ones behind the barriers. And that's when we really come to know and love each other and grow together the way Heavenly Father wants us to. If there are barriers in your marriage relationship, try to work together to take them down. It will be worth the risk. Besides, that police barricade looked like a lot of hot, sweaty work. Who needs that?

I never did find out why that police barricade was there. I didn't hear anything on the news about an ax murderer in my neighborhood, so that's good. I still wonder about it, though.

54

For Better or for Worse — Talk about the Better

"For better or for worse" is a phrase commonly used in marriage ceremonies to describe our commitment to each other under any circumstance. Sadly, though, this phrase is also used as a bumper-sticker reply to the challenging parts of marriage. If you're struggling with the loss of a job, poor health, or difficulties with extended family, you may hear, "Well, it *is* for better or for worse," to remind you of what you took on. As if, on top of everything else you're dealing with, you need to be brought to task on your wedding vows.

We will all face challenges in our marriages, and we will hopefully learn ways to seek strength from our commitment to each other. But do we need to take a part of those traditional wedding vows and turn it into a battering ram to use on each other in our low moments? (Okay, so maybe I've heard this one too many times.) Instead, let's take this phrase and allow it to remind us of the better parts of our marriage. Focus on the good parts, the happy moments you share, the times that remind you why you're together. As challenges come, look to what you learned, what has strengthened your relationship. If you do this, the better will outweigh the worse, so much so that it will become what you talk about to others. And when people share with you the challenges they are facing, offer them something that will really help—your faith that the *better* will come.

55

Pulling Together

Wells Barney was an award-winning horse trainer who happened to be my husband's cousin. He spent his life training draft horses and especially enjoyed horse-pulling competitions, where two draft horses pulling together move enormous amounts of weight. Wells has passed on, but each year people from all over the country gather at the Rigby Rodeo Grounds in Idaho for the Wells Barney Memorial Horse Pull. Wells came to my home several times, always bringing horse-training tales and plenty of laughter. I miss him. He told me once that I reminded him of his wife, who had passed away several years before. It was one of the highest compliments I've ever received.

At a recent temple wedding I attended, the sealer was an older rancher who reminded me of Wells. His advice to the young couple being married was filled with images of land and animals—his life teachers. Then, to the apparent surprise of everyone in the room, he compared the couple to two draft horses, ready to pull a heavy load, yoked with the love of the Savior. While some people found humor and some winced at the unflattering comparison between this shiny bride and groom and a pair of sweaty draft horses heaving a pile of stone, tears filled my eyes. I knew exactly what the sealer was talking about, and I couldn't think of a more perfect image of what this couple, sealed by the Savior, will eventually do together.

Perhaps you've already seen for yourselves a pair of powerful, majestic Clydesdales or Belgians or Percherons or Shires standing equally yoked, eyes locked on their future, their strength as one pulling against the load they carry. If you have, you may not mind the comparison so much. A team of draft horses is simply magnificent.

Like these horses, you and your wife or husband will need to pull heavy loads throughout your lives. It will be easier and better if you do it together. As strong as they are, each draft horse in a pair can only pull a limited amount of weight alone. But together they can pull not just double the individual amount, but hundreds or even thousands of pounds more. So can you and your wife or husband. Keep this image in your mind as the two of you face challenges. Stand equally yoked by the Savior's love, your eyes steady on the future, and pull together.

56

And Just to Be on the Safe Side

In this book's introduction, I mentioned a General Authority who had yet to learn to pick up his socks. He referred us to a book to solve these marriage challenges. Since this is such a book, I will do the honors: pick up your socks.

Yet I have been married for thirty-one years, and I still leave my shoes all over the house. My thoughtful husband has built beautiful shoe racks in our closet, subtle enticements to help me improve this bad habit. It hasn't worked. My shoes are everywhere. Perhaps for such marriage woes as socks and shoes, even a book can't cut it. You're on your own with this one.

Your Thoughts

Your Thoughts

_____

_____

_____

_____

_____

_____

_____

_____

_____

_____

_____

_____

_____

_____

_____

_____

_____

_____

_____

_____

_____

Your Thoughts

About the Author

Amy Martinsen received a bachelor of arts in English education from Arizona State University, and a master of arts in English from Northern Arizona University. She wrote the novels *Changing Worlds* (2015) and *The Secret Obituary Writer* (2016), both of which were published by Walnut Springs Press. *The Secret Obituary Writer* was nominated for a 2016 Whitney Award. In 2017, a popular blogger selected Amy as one of the Top Ten LDS Authors You Need to Read. Amy brings a variety of insights to her writing, including a marriage of over three decades, raising five children, and serving in many Church leadership positions. In addition, she is the author of the short story "Lilly's Photograph" (Moose Enterprise, 2002), and "The Tower of Babel and the Teaching of Grammar: Writing Instruction for a New Century," published in the September 2000 *English Journal*. Readers can learn more about Amy and her books at goawayimreading.com.